B48 846 846 0

KT-558-296

WILD about

SUPERBIKES

By Jeff Painter and Richard Newland

Stats and Facts • Top makes • Top models • Top speeds

WILD about

SUPERBIKES

ROTHERHAM LIBRARY &
INFORMATION SERVICES

J629.22

B48 846 846 0

R0000064110

Copyright © *ticktock* Entertainment Ltd 2004
First published in Great Britain in 2003 by *ticktock* Media Ltd.,
Unit 2, Orchard Business Centre, North Farm Road, Tunbridge Wells, Kent, TN2 3XF
We would like to thank: Jamie Asher, Richard Newland of Fast Bikes magazine and Elizabeth Wiggans.
All images Car Photo Library - www.carphoto.co.uk.
ISBN 1 86007 361 1 HB
ISBN 1 86007 367 0 PB
Printed in China
A CIP catalogue record for this book is available from the British Library.
All rights reserved. No part of this publication may be reproduced, copied,
stored in a retrieval system, or transmitted in any form or by any means
electronic, mechanical, photocopying, recording or otherwise without prior
written permission of the copyright owner.

CONTENTS

APRILIA RSV MILLE R

The Italian company Aprilia first became known as a maker of bicycles. Then, in 1968, they began producing motorcycles and mopeds. In 2002, Aprilia launched the Mille R. This beautiful machine is big, fast and very comfortable to ride. The 'R' stands for racing, as this bike is the fastest machine Aprilia have ever made.

DID YOU KNOW?

'Mille' is the Italian word for 'one thousand'. The RSV is called a 'Mille' because the engine is almost 1000 cc.

Up until the end of 2001, all Mille R's were single seat bikes. Then in 2002 Aprilia made a two seater version.

One of the most eye-catching features of the Aprilia is its triple **headlight**.

STATS AND FACTS

LAUNCHED: *2002*

ORIGIN: *Italy*

ENGINE: *997.6 cc*

CYLINDERS: *2*

MAX POWER: *128 bhp at 9,500 rpm*

MAX TORQUE: *101 NM at 7,400 rpm*

GEARS: *6*

DRY WEIGHT: *168 kg*

MAX SPEED: *168 mph*

FUEL TANK CAPACITY: *18 litres*

COLOURS: *Aprilia Black or Flashy Yellow*

COST: *£9,999*

The new Mille has special **radial brakes** at the front. These are much stronger than normal brakes, so the bike can stop very quickly if it needs to.

BENELLI TORNADO

This Italian company was founded in 1911 by a widow called Teresa Benelli. She started the business to provide jobs for her six sons. The Benelli Mechanical Workshop started off making spare parts for cars and motorcycles. Then in 1921 the company made their first motorcycle. In 2002 Benelli started selling the Tornado, a 162 mph **superbike**.

The Tornado's **engine** is also used as part of the bike's **frame**. This makes the bike stronger.

DID YOU KNOW?

The Benelli is built in Italy. But it was designed by an Englishman, and uses suspension made in Sweden.

The Tornado's **radiator** is under the seat. Two big **fans** suck in air to cool the radiator.

STATS AND FACTS

LAUNCHED: *2002*

ORIGIN: *Italy*

ENGINE: *898 cc*

CYLINDERS: *3*

MAX POWER: *147 bhp at 11,500 rpm*

MAX TORQUE: *100 NM at 8,500 rpm*

GEARS: *6*

DRY WEIGHT: *185 kg*

MAX SPEED: *162 mph (est)*

FUEL TANK CAPACITY: *18 litres*

COLOURS: *Green/Silver*

COST: *£22,000*

A more powerful, racing version of the Tornado has competed at the World Superbike Championships. It was designed by Italian Riccardo Rosa, who has worked with the Italian car company Ferrari.

BUELL XB9R FIREBOLT

Buell was formed in 1993 by a man called Erik Buell. He set up the company with help from the famous American motorcycle company Harley-Davidson (*see p16-17*). Harley-Davidson are not known for making fast bikes. But Buell had the idea of using a Harley **engine** in a lighter bike to make a really fast machine.

DID YOU KNOW?

Weighing just 175 kgs, the Firebolt is one of the lightest superbikes in the world.

The Firebolt has a belt instead of a chain to make the back wheel go round.

The Firebolt has **perimeter brakes** at the front. The brake disc is much bigger than normal, which means you can stop quicker.

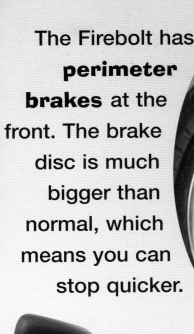

LAUNCHED: *2002*

ORIGIN: *USA*

ENGINE: *984 cc*

CYLINDERS: *2*

MAX POWER: *92 bhp at 7,200 rpm*

MAX TORQUE: *92 NM at 5,500 rpm*

GEARS: *5*

DRY WEIGHT: *175 kg*

MAX SPEED: *130 mph (est)*

FUEL TANK CAPACITY: *14 litres*

COLOURS: *Arctic White, Battle Blue*

COST: *£7,345*

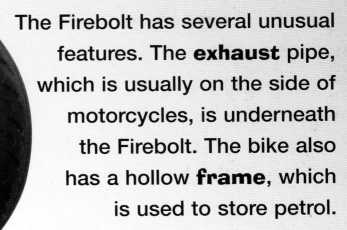

The Firebolt has several unusual features. The **exhaust** pipe, which is usually on the side of motorcycles, is underneath the Firebolt. The bike also has a hollow **frame**, which is used to store petrol.

HONDA CBR1100XX BLACKBIRD

The Japanese firm Honda is one of the biggest motorcycle makers in the world. The Blackbird used to be the fastest motorcycle in the world, until Suzuki built the Hayabusa *(see p24-25)*. With a few tweaks, the Blackbird can rocket to an incredible 200 mph.

DID YOU KNOW?

In 2001, a rider on a turbo-charged Blackbird did a wheelie at an amazing 200 mph!

The Blackbird has **linked brakes**. When you pull the front brake lever the back brake works too - and when you push the back brake pedal the front brake works as well.

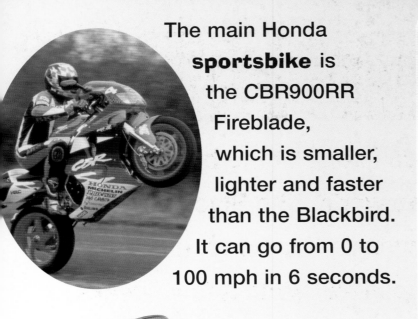

The main Honda **sportsbike** is the CBR900RR Fireblade, which is smaller, lighter and faster than the Blackbird. It can go from 0 to 100 mph in 6 seconds.

STATS AND FACTS

LAUNCHED: *1996*

ORIGIN: *Japan*

ENGINE: *1,137 cc*

CYLINDERS: *4*

MAX POWER: *164 bhp at 9,200 rpm*

MAX TORQUE: *116 NM at 7,300 rpm*

GEARS: *6*

DRY WEIGHT: *223 kg*

MAX SPEED: *174 mph*

FUEL TANK CAPACITY: *24 litres*

COLOURS: *Black, Blue, Red*

COST: *£10,349*

The Blackbird's **acceleration** is awesome. Thanks to its streamlined shape and huge **engine**, this bike can race from 0 to 130 mph in just 11 seconds.

KAWASAKI NINJA ZX-12R

The Japanese company Kawasaki have always made very fast motorcycles. The ZX-12R is the fastest bike on the planet, capable of just under 200 mph. The Ninja also has a big fuel **tank**, which means you can ride it long distances without stopping.

The ZX-12R has such good **brakes** that it is able to go from 70 mph to a stop in under 4 seconds.

The scoop under the **headlight** forces air into the **engine**, which drags extra fuel in. This gives the ZX-12R even more power.

DID YOU KNOW?

The ZX-12R has the widest back tyre of any sportsbike. It is a massive 200 mm wide!

STATS AND FACTS

LAUNCHED: *2000*

ORIGIN: *Japan*

ENGINE: *1,199 cc*

CYLINDERS: *4*

MAX POWER: *165 bhp at 9,800 rpm*

MAX TORQUE: *130 NM at 7,800*

GEARS: *6*

DRY WEIGHT: *210 kg*

MAX SPEED: *190 mph*

FUEL TANK CAPACITY: *20 litres*

COLOURS: *Black/Gold, Silver, Kawasaki Green*

COST: *£9,315*

The ZX-12R's **fairing** was made with help from Kawasaki's aircraft division. It was designed to make the bike as **aerodynamic** as possible.

MONDIAL PIEGA

Mondial was founded by an Italian called Earls Boselli. His bikes won lots of races, especially in the 1940s and 1950s. The company went out of business in 1967, but in 1997 they started making motorcycles again. The Piega is the first new Mondial in 30 years.

The **engine** in the Mondial is not Italian like the rest of the bike. It is Japanese, and was first used in a Honda motorcycle.

DID YOU KNOW?

The new owners of Mondial had never made motorcycles before buying the company. The Piega was their first bike.

The Mondial Piega has special **radial brakes.** They are stronger than ordinary brakes, and slow this fiery bike down in record time.

STATS AND FACTS

LAUNCHED: *2002*

ORIGIN: *Italy*

ENGINE: *999 cc*

CYLINDERS: *2*

MAX POWER: *140 bhp at 9,800 rpm*

MAX TORQUE: *100 NM at 8,800 rpm*

GEARS: *6*

DRY WEIGHT: *226 kg*

MAX SPEED: *161 mph*

FUEL TANK CAPACITY: *20 litres*

COLOURS: *Silver, Blue*

COST: *£15,500*

The Piega's **fairing** is made from **carbon fibre**, and is only available in silver and blue.

HARLEY V-ROD

Famous for being the bikes that Hell's Angels like to ride, the Harley-Davidson has always been a bike for cruising on. There are lots of straight roads in America, and Harleys were made to ride long distances in comfort. However, the V-Rod is much sportier than other Harleys. It is the fastest bike the company have ever made.

DID YOU KNOW?

Despite being heavy motorcycles, the famous stunt rider Evel Knievel did all his jumps on a Harley-Davidson.

The V-Rod's fuel **tank** is under the seat. The space this saves leaves room for **air intakes**. These force more fuel into the bike's engine, supplying the V-Rod with extra power.

There is a special badge on the V-Rod's tank. It says that the Harley-Davidson company have been making bikes for one hundred years.

The V-Rod has a brand new water-cooled **engine**. It was designed with the German sports car maker Porsche.

CAGIVA V-RAPTOR 1000

DID YOU KNOW?

The name Cagiva is made up of 2 letters from the founder's surname and first name – Ca(stiglioni) Gi(ovanni) – and the first 2 letters of the company's hometown – Va(rese).

The Cagiva company built their first two motorcycles in 1978. A year later, they were building over 40,000 bikes a year. This mad-looking machine was designed for the company by the Italian Miguel Galluzzi.

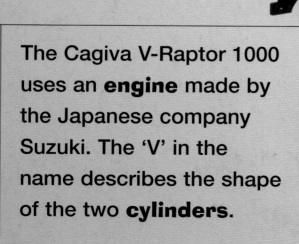

The Cagiva V-Raptor 1000 uses an **engine** made by the Japanese company Suzuki. The 'V' in the name describes the shape of the two **cylinders**.

This bike has claws! The V-Raptor has a strange set of talons by the passenger footrest.

STATS AND FACTS

LAUNCHED: *2000*

ORIGIN: *Italy*

ENGINE: *996 cc*

CYLINDERS: *2*

MAX POWER: *114 bhp at 8,500 rpm*

MAX TORQUE: *96 NM at 7,000 rpm*

GEARS: *6*

DRY WEIGHT: *197 kg*

MAX SPEED: *149 mph*

FUEL TANK CAPACITY: *18 litres*

COLOUR: *Red*

COST: *£7,149*

The bike is a 'Naked' sportbike. This means that there is no **bodywork**, or **fairing**, covering the engine.

DUCATI 999R

DID YOU KNOW?

The 'R' is based on the same bike that is raced in the World Superbike series.

Ducati are an Italian motorbike company. The 999 is the fastest and most expensive Ducati. It comes in three versions – the 999, 999S and 999R. The 'R' is the fastest of the bikes, and is made of **carbon fibre** and **aluminium**.

This is a Ducati 749. It looks almost exactly the same as the 999R, but it has a 749 cc **engine**. This means it has less power and is a bit slower.

The 999R's seat and fuel **tank** can be moved backwards and forwards, and the footrests can be moved up and down. This Ducati can be made comfortable to ride, however tall or short you are.

STATS AND FACTS

LAUNCHED: *2002*

ORIGIN: *Italy*

ENGINE: *999 cc*

CYLINDERS: *2*

MAX POWER: *139 bhp at 10,000 rpm*

MAX TORQUE: *108 NM at 8,000 rpm*

GEARS: *6*

DRY WEIGHT: *193 kg*

MAX SPEED: *175 mph (est)*

FUEL TANK CAPACITY: *15.5 litres*

COLOURS: *Red or Yellow*

COST: *£19,300*

Each 999R has a unique silver badge to prove that it is a limited edition bike.

MV AGUSTA F4 SPR SENNA

MV Agusta is another Italian company with a racing history. Agusta bikes won 270 Grand Prix between 1950–1975 before the company ran out of money and closed. Then, in 1999, MV Agusta was brought back to life with the launch of the stunning F4. Lots of people think the Senna is the most beautiful bike in the world.

The Senna's **exhausts** come out under the seat, rather than at the side of the bike.

DID YOU KNOW?

Whenever a MV F4 Senna is sold, some of the money is given to educate Brazilian children.

The Senna's twin **headlights** are arranged on top of each other. This makes the front of the bike more **aerodynamic**.

STATS AND FACTS

LAUNCHED: 2002

ORIGIN: Italy

ENGINE: 749 cc

CYLINDERS: 4

MAX POWER: 140 bhp at 12,600 rpm

MAX TORQUE: 81 NM at 10,500 rpm

GEARS: 6

DRY WEIGHT: 188 kg

MAX SPEED: 177 mph

FUEL TANK CAPACITY: 20 litres

COLOURS: Grey and Red

COST: £17,350

The Senna was made in memory of the famous Formula 1 racing driver Ayrton Senna. Only 300 were made.

SUZUKI GSX 1300R HAYABUSA

The Japanese bike maker Suzuki was formed in 1952. In 1998 they built a new motorcycle called the Hayabusa. At the time, the Hayabusa was the fastest bike in the world. This monster's **engine** is actually bigger than those found in many cars.

DID YOU KNOW?

A Hayabusa is so powerful that it can wear out a back tyre in as little as a thousand miles.

The GSX-R100 is the smaller brother of the Hayabusa. The top speed is the same as the Hayabusa, but this bike has better **acceleration** because it is lighter.

The British Land Speed Record for a motorcycle is held by a **turbo-charged** Hayabusa. This bike reached a speed in excess of 241 mph!

STATS AND FACTS

LAUNCHED: *1998*

ORIGIN: *Japan*

ENGINE: *1,298 cc*

CYLINDERS: *4*

MAX POWER: *155 bhp at 9,000 rpm*

MAX TORQUE: *134 NM at 6,800 rpm*

GEARS: *6*

DRY WEIGHT: *215 kg*

MAX SPEED: *186 mph*

FUEL TANK CAPACITY: *18 litres*

COLOURS: *Blue & Black, Blue & Silver, Silver*

COST: *£8,299*

The Hayabusa is a Japanese bird of prey that eats blackbirds. Suzuki called their new **superbike** a Hayabusa because it is faster and more powerful than Honda's CBR1100XX Blackbird (*see p10-11*), its main rival.

TRIUMPH DAYTONA 955i

Triumph is one of the oldest motorcycle companies still running today. It was founded in 1902. The Daytona 955i is the only British sports bike that can keep up with the fastest Japanese and Italian bikes. It was first made in 1997, but several new versions have appeared since.

This is the Triumph Speed-Twin. It was first made in 1937, and models continued to be made for over 20 years. The Speed-Twin also inspired the Bonneville, one of the most popular bikes of the 1950s.

Whilst the Triumph is very powerful, it is also quite heavy. It weighs 20 kg more than one of its rivals, the Honda Fireblade (*see p11*).

The Daytona has a 'naked' brother called the Speed Triple. It has the same **engine** and **chassis**, but it has no **fairing**.

STATS AND FACTS

LAUNCHED: *1997*

ORIGIN: *UK*

ENGINE: *955 cc*

CYLINDERS: *3*

MAX POWER: *147 bhp at 10,700 rpm*

MAX TORQUE: *100 NM at 8,200 rpm*

GEARS: *6*

DRY WEIGHT: *191 kg*

MAX SPEED: *165 mph*

FUEL TANK CAPACITY: *21 litres*

COLOURS: *Jet Black, Acidic Yellow, Tornado Red*

COST: *£8,799*

DID YOU KNOW?

A Daytona was featured in "Mission Impossible 2", starring Tom Cruise.

YAMAHA YZF R1

The Yamaha Motor Company is one of the best known motorcycle producers in the world. Originally a maker of musical instruments, the firm started to make motorcycle after the Second World War. In 2002 Yamaha launched the latest version of their incredibly successful R1 bike, which has competed in the British Superbike Championship.

DID YOU KNOW?

The Yamaha R1 will do over 75 mph in first gear, and over 100 mph in second gear.

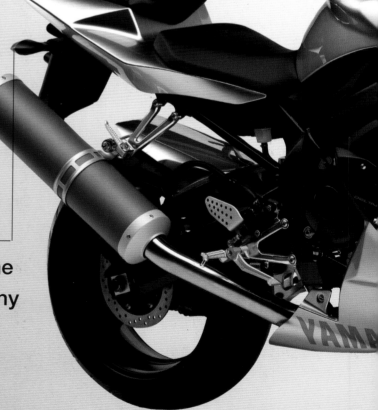

The R1 has no light bulbs at the back. Instead it is fitted with tiny **LEDs** (Light Emitting Diodes). If one stops working, there are still another 20 providing light.

One of Yamaha's most popular bikes is the YZF-R6. It isn't as fast as an R1. But because it is small and light it can keep up with most bigger bikes on twisty racetracks and roads.

STATS AND FACTS

LAUNCHED: *2002*

ORIGIN: *Japan*

ENGINE: *998 cc*

CYLINDERS: *4*

MAX POWER: *152 bhp at 10,500 rpm*

MAX TORQUE: *107 NM at 8,500 rpm*

GEARS: *6*

DRY WEIGHT: *174 kg*

MAX SPEED: *176 mph*

FUEL TANK CAPACITY: *18 litres*

COLOURS: *Blue, Red, White*

COST: *£9,134*

To make the new R1 even quicker, Yamaha have given it a lighter **chassis** and wheels. The front and back of the bike are also more pointed and **aerodynamic**.

GLOSSARY

ACCELERATION Making a bike go faster by opening the throttle.

AERODYNAMIC A shape that cuts through the air around it.

AIR INTAKES Large scoops that direct air into the engine, sucking in extra fuel to give a bike more power.

ALUMINIUM A lightweight, but strong, metal.

BHP Brake horse power, the usual measure of an engine's power.

BODYWORK Plastic panels which cover the chassis and engine.

BRAKES Part of a bike used to slow it down.

CARBON FIBRE A very light, but strong, material.

CC Cubic capacity, the measurement used for the size of the engine.

CHASSIS *See Frame.*

CYLINDER The part of the engine where fuel is burned to make energy.

ENGINE The part of the bike where the fuel is burned to create energy.

EXHAUST Pipe at the back of the bike where poisonous gases made when petrol is burned are let out. The exhaust is also used to reduce engine noise.

FAIRING The front and side parts of the bodywork.

FANS Part of the bike that pushes or pulls cool air through the radiator, helping to cool the engine.

FORKS The fork-shaped tubes that hold the front wheel and handlebars in place.

FRAME The part of the bike which holds the engine, wheels and bodywork together. Sometimes called the chassis.

GEARS System that lets a bike go faster or slower without damaging the engine.

HEADLIGHT The bright light at the front of the bike.

LED Light Emitting Diode, a source of light used in some brake lights.

LINKED BRAKES System where the front brake lever also works the back brake, and the back brake lever works the front brake.

PERIMETER BRAKES Braking system where the brake disc is mounted round the edge of the wheel.

RADIAL BRAKES Braking system where the brake discs are mounted at the bottom of the forks, parallel to the wheel.

RADIATOR Part of the bike that uses water to stop the engine from overheating.

RPM Revolutions (revs) of the engine per minute.

SPORTSBIKE A fast motorcycle that has been developed for road use.

SUPERBIKE A fast motorcycle that is very similar to a race bike.

SUSPENSION Springs and shock absorbers attached to a bike's wheels, giving a smooth ride in spite of bumps in the road.

TANK Hollow metal unit where petrol is stored.

THROTTLE The part of a bike that is used to make it go faster or slower.

TORQUE AND NM The measurements for an engine's power.

TURBO System that increases a bike's power by forcing more air into the engine.

TYRE A rubber covering for a wheel, filled with compressed air.

INDEX